Matthew 14:13–21;
Mark 6:30–44;
Luke 9:10–17;
John 6:1–14 for Children

Written by Joanne Bader
Illustrated by Michael Streff

Jesus and His followers
Had traveled far and wide.
They came across a quiet sea
And climbed the mountainside.

Jesus would have liked to rest
From work that He had done,
But crowds of people followed Him
And joined Him in the sun.

The people loved to hear Him preach.
They shouted, "Tell us more!"
Some hoped to see the miracles
They knew He'd done before.

He welcomed them and spoke to them
About the Word of God.
He healed all those who needed it
With just a gentle nod.

When evening came they searched for food,
But the disciples said,
"Let's send them home or into town
To eat and go to bed."

"They do not need to go away,"
Our Lord replied so calmly.
"You give them something they can eat—
For this crowd is quite hungry."

At last one of the Twelve spoke up
To tell what he had found.
He told the others that a boy
Had food to pass around.

"Well, just what is it?" they all asked.
"How many will it feed?
We must do something here and now."
On that they all agreed!

"It's not much food to feed this crowd,"
The one disciple said.
"He only has two fish to eat
And five small loaves of bread."

Then Jesus spoke, "Bring it to Me;
Seat people on the ground."
He took the food and then gave thanks
And handed it around.

Each lady, man, and child, in turn,
Took some and passed it on.
They ate and ate and ate lots more.
The food still was not gone.

Now Jesus gave them this command,
"You've had enough to eat,
So gather pieces that are left
Of barley loaves and meat."

They filled 12 baskets with the crumbs
Too big to throw away.
Five thousand men plus moms and kids
Were fed by God that day.

God cares for us as He did them.
He gives us all we need.
He blesses us with food and drink.
These gifts are guaranteed.

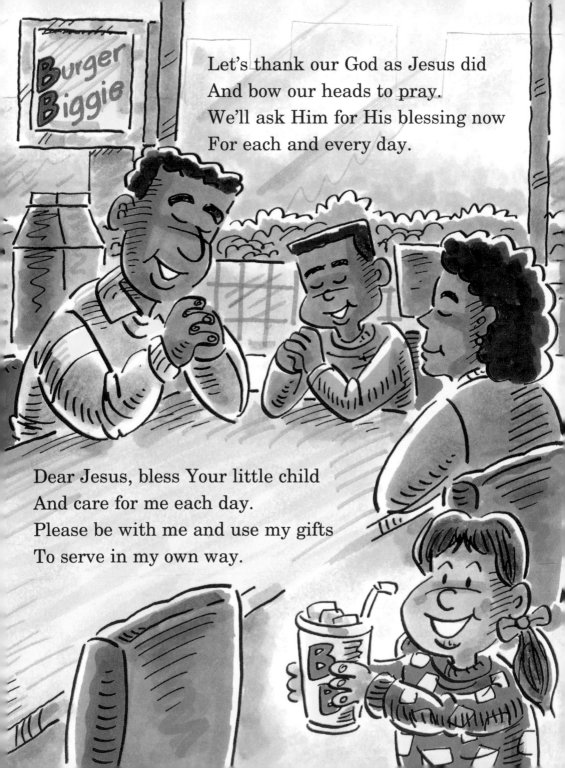

Let's thank our God as Jesus did
And bow our heads to pray.
We'll ask Him for His blessing now
For each and every day.

Dear Jesus, bless Your little child
And care for me each day.
Please be with me and use my gifts
To serve in my own way.

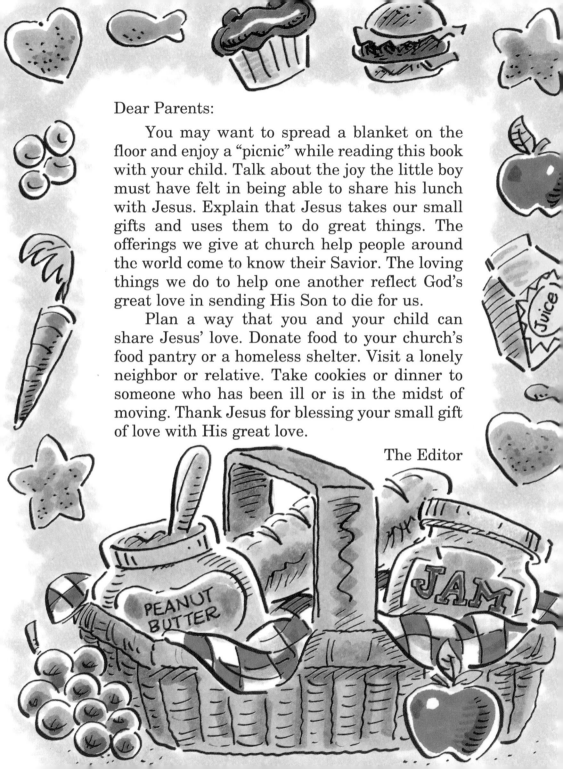

Dear Parents:

You may want to spread a blanket on the floor and enjoy a "picnic" while reading this book with your child. Talk about the joy the little boy must have felt in being able to share his lunch with Jesus. Explain that Jesus takes our small gifts and uses them to do great things. The offerings we give at church help people around the world come to know their Savior. The loving things we do to help one another reflect God's great love in sending His Son to die for us.

Plan a way that you and your child can share Jesus' love. Donate food to your church's food pantry or a homeless shelter. Visit a lonely neighbor or relative. Take cookies or dinner to someone who has been ill or is in the midst of moving. Thank Jesus for blessing your small gift of love with His great love.

The Editor